DENNIS ADAMS

THE ARCHITECTURE OF AMNESIA

For Jody and Todd

DENNIS ADAMS

THE ARCHITECTURE OF AMNESIA

Essay by

Mary Anne Staniszewski

KENT

Frank Lloyd Wright, Imperial Hotel, Tokyo, in demolition, 1968. Photo: Edgar Tafel

The Earthquake and the Corporation

February 28, 1968, Tokyo. The last fragments of Frank Lloyd Wright's Imperial Hotel were bulldozed to make way for a more economically efficient seventeen-story hotel. Preservationist campaigns had proved futile. The Imperial's specially designed furnishings (including Wright's Peacock Chairs, which sold for one dollar each) were peddled at a department store as second-hand merchandise.

That this great structure could not withstand the demands of late capitalist corporate accounting is particularly ironic considering the history of the building. On the Imperial's opening day, September 1, 1923, Tokyo had been hit with the most severe earthquake in Japan since the turn of the century. The hotel suffered only minor damage, and it withstood twenty-four more hours of aftershock and conflagration. The building then survived World War II intact.

Yet art and architectural institutions did nothing to save this masterpiece of modernist architecture. (When Wright himself was asked in 1923 what he had done that was worthy of special mention, he answered, "The Imperial Hotel of Tokyo, Japan, and 176 other buildings of note.")[1] The Museum of Modern Art, for example, was not interested in mementos from the Imperial because, according to MoMA's curator of architecture and design, Arthur Drexler, they would have made "no sense taken out of context."[2]

The Peace Tower and the City of Angels

The Peace Tower, 1966 (*Art in America* cover, November/December 1971)

Spring 1966, Los Angeles. On an empty lot, on the crest of the hill where the Sunset Strip intersects La Cienega Boulevard, a fifty-eight-foot steel tower was erected. The tower stood in front of a one-hundred-foot billboard studded with panels donated by more than four hundred artists from around the world. At the opening ceremony, Susan Sontag gave a speech and read a telegram of "solidarité totale" from a contingent of French artists and intellectuals that included Simone de Beauvoir, André Breton, André Masson, and Jean-Paul Sartre. This was the Peace Tower Project. Produced by the Los Angeles Artists Protest Committee and organized by Irving Petlin (the actual tower was designed by Mark di Suvero), the Peace Tower was one of the earliest and most visible demonstrations against the United States involvement in Vietnam.

The Peace Tower stood for three months. Spotlit at night, the lot was guarded around the clock. The site became a magnet for the local community during its construction and throughout the three months. According to some accounts, there were days when as many as one thousand people gathered. The crowds included sheriffs, Hell's Angels, artists, military personnel, and passersby. Young blacks from the Watts district volunteered as additional guards. A group of Hollywood writers who had been blacklisted during the McCarthy years donated their support. The agitprop tower became the centerpiece for real-life street theater. It successfully rearranged the social geography of Los Angeles, using avant-garde strategies to address political issues.

When it was erected, the Peace Tower had a powerful impact. The event was picked up by the international press and for several weeks was regularly covered by the local television stations. But not one of the historical accounts of the art and culture of the sixties even mentions this paradigm of avant-garde activism.

Toppled Heads and Colonies

1962, Algiers. As the defeated French government scrambled to divest itself of 130 years of colonial rule, the Palais d'Eté in Algiers was stripped of eight statues of French military governors. These symbols of French colonial authority were shipped back to France and are now kept in relative obscurity. (They have been relegated to the status of monuments to local heroes and are on display in places like the park in the hometown of one of the governors, the military school attended by another, and another's family estate.) The incident, an expelled regime's attempt to save face, exemplifies the rearrangement of public monuments and collective memory that comes in the wake of revolution or with a change in political authority.

Memories and Modern Art

Dennis Adams has used photographs of the dismantling of the French-Algerian statues in his investigation of issues dealing with collective memory. I use the term "collective memory," rather than "history," to suggest a remembrance of things past that exists as recollections of individuals. Traditionally, history is affiliated with ideological closure and functions as recorded truth; collective memory suggests a reconstruction of the past that is disseminated within a population limited by prejudices, shaped by contexts, and continuously changing with time. And unlike traditional history, which is a selective representation of great events and master accomplishments, collective memory spans the spectrum of experience, from our most famous monuments to the overlooked signposts of everyday life. It's simply history that circulates as memory. As Adams has said, he is "interested in the history of the last forty years. It's still tied to living bodies, people still have a vested interest in it. . . . It is always recent history that is the most manipulated."[3]

Cover from a Situationist journal, 1959; altered map of France with Algerian cities replacing French cities

Since the summer of 1988 Adams has been working on a series of site-specific projects in France dealing with the Algerian War of Independence—a memory that remains somewhat dysfunctional for the French.[4] The enforcement of this cultural amnesia surfaced when Adams was invited to create a public art project for the city of Dijon. When city officials were informed that the artist planned to recontextualize photographs of the Algerian colonial experience, they rejected the proposal as too controversial. The project has never been realized.

"My idea was to crack the silence. I wanted to touch the subject of the war through a public intervention that went straight to the nerves," says Adams. He proposed constructing an "alternative" monument at the entrance to Dijon's ceremonial thoroughfare, the boulevard Charles de Gaulle (an appropriate avenue considering that de Gaulle used the Algerian conflict as a political instrument to consolidate his power). Adams planned to erect a replica of the old cast-concrete public pissoirs that are still found throughout the city in small numbers (two of them flank the other end of the boulevard Charles de Gaulle). The walls of the replica would have been double the thickness of the original pavilions (which would have emphasized their "bunkerlike" appearance, according to the artist) and inside, where one would expect to find urinal niches, there would have been backlit photographic transparencies taken in Algeria in 1962 of the dismantled statues of the French military governors.

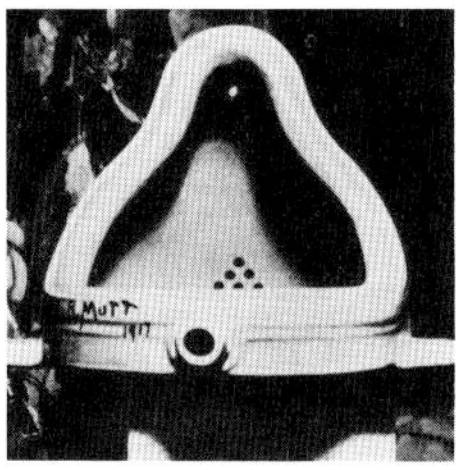
Marcel Duchamp, *Fountain* (readymade), 1917

The Dijon project has obvious "aesthetic" references to Duchamp's readymades. This might also lead the viewer to remember that the readymades were among the first modern works of art to show the way our representations—including our most "original" creations—are shaped by the conventions of culture and the limits of a particular history.[5] But Adams had also wanted the Dijon project to deal with "exclusively masculine spaces" and "male conventions," an apt frame of reference for a project dealing with modern European imperialism. The actual pissoirs found on the streets of Dijon were constructed over thirty years ago and are "not tied to the body of the contemporary city, but are figures of another, earlier language." They are what Adams describes as "urban anachronisms." They are already instruments of memory.

What may appear to be an irreverent Dada jest is in fact an attempt to make visible the intersection of high European colonialism,[6] high modernism, and patriarchy, institutions that share a similar trajectory and that have undergone radical dissolution since the end of World War II. The Dijon project would have recast one of the most undisguised examples of segregated masculine space as public domain. (Isn't it interesting that only men have traditionally been provided with these types of facilities? What does this imply about the territory of the street?) Opening a pissoir to the entire population would have symbolically dismantled the acceptance of the masculine as the neutral standard—an effective strategy for a project that would have tampered with the public memory of its recent colonialist past, considering that Western imperialist authority was founded upon the sovereignty of a white, patriarchal world view.

Adams's insistence on creating ephemeral public projects also challenges, on a fundamental level, modern art's valorization of patriarchal property rights (taking into account, of course, that in order for anything in our culture to be valued and have meaning, it must be subject to the laws of property and exchange). Modernism was founded upon a belief in the modern subject's two fundamental rights of owning property and exchanging goods, rights that, until quite recently, have been a predominantly masculine privilege. Adams's Dijon proposal is part of an ongoing series in which he uses a critique of high modernism and patriarchal privilege to expose the ideological license and wide-reaching implications of European colonialism.

Adams's 1989 installation at the Musée d'Art Moderne in Paris transposed the questions associated with the Dijon project to the modern art museum. He constructed a partial wall, suspended approximately two and a half feet off the ground, that divided a glass-fronted gallery located at the museum's entrance. Four of the collection's abstract paintings—all produced during the years of the Algerian war—were mounted on the front of the partition, duplicating the way they had been installed in the museum. (The artist considered this painting installation a "readymade.") From behind the partition, Adams projected a panoramic image of Algerian women and children running toward the camera during a street demonstration for Algerian independence. The floor of the space was covered with mirrored panels, intended, according to the artist, to create an unsettling sense of dislocation. Adams had the gallery locked during the installation, so that from outside the room, looking through its glass facade, viewers saw the partition with the modernist masterworks and, below them, reflected in the mirrored floor, the projected images documenting the dissolution of French colonial power. The installation functioned as an architectural metaphor, destabilizing the museum's authority as a repository of official history and culture. It worked, in a sense, to make the political unconscious of the museum visible.

Barbara Kruger, *Untitled* (You construct intricate rituals which allow you to touch the skin of other men), 1980. Courtesy: Mary Boone Gallery, NY

European high modernism and high colonialism share similar ideological presuppositions, as well as the same historical berth. High modernism was founded upon the faith that Western culture could provide a universal language for the modern world. European colonialism was an attempt to reshape the world according to Western patriarchal standards. Both were consolidated in the nineteenth century, flourished during the first half of this century, and have undergone widespread dissolution since World War II. But in response to this dissolution, some of their most exaggerated manifestations—Abstract Expressionism and apartheid, for example—exist as post–World War II phenomena. (It is now well known that Abstract Expressionism became an instrument of the Cold War when it was exported abroad under the auspices of the Museum of Modern Art and the Central Intelligence Agency as a symbol of American freedom of expression.) In the Musée d'Art Moderne installation, Adams subverted "official collective memory" in what is traditionally seen as a neutral social space and challenged the viewer's perception of these abstract paintings as autonomous and purely aesthetic treasures of modern culture.

During the past year Adams has continued to work with the official monuments and the collective memory of France and Algeria. In 1989, he saw the international exhibition *Magiciens de la Terre* (which has generally been received as a failed attempt to exhibit the work of Third World and Western artists together and to treat non-Western culture with sensitivity and respect) as another potentially colonialist spectacle where cultural diversity is leveled and all the contributions are evaluated according to Western standards. As an internal critique of this enterprise, he mounted the photographs of the statues from the Palais d'Eté onto a flatbed truck he parked in front of the entrance of the Parc La Villette, one of the two sites for the exhibition and where many of these trucks were being used for the ongoing construction of the park. (Adams's use of the truck, which is, of course, a vehicle of transport, could be read as an allusion to the shipment of the military governor statues back to France.)

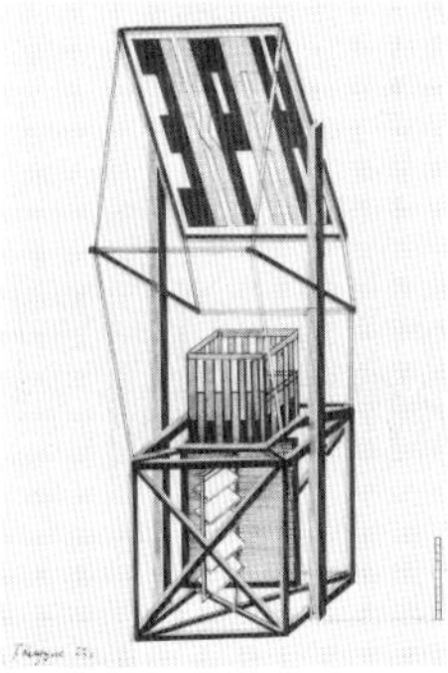

G.G. Klucis, *Design for Screen*, 1922

Adams's work participates in the modern tradition of the avant-garde, specifically the post–World War II avant-garde, which reevaluated the strategies of the "historical avant-garde" of the teens, twenties, and thirties: Dada, Surrealism, the Bauhaus, and the Soviet Project, for example. (By avant-garde, I mean work that rejects autonomous art whose function and validity are determined solely by aesthetic criteria, that is, work that rejects modernism.) The historical avant-garde believed that art would be an instrument of radical social reform, but the postwar avant-garde has modified their predecessors' utopian agendas. Similar to contemporary representatives of the postwar avant-garde like Hans Haacke, Barbara Kruger, Antonio Muntadas, and Krzysztof Wodiczko, Adams uses aesthetic venues to stage social critiques that make visible the intersection of aesthetic and nonaesthetic institutions of power.

Hans Haacke, *And You Were Victorious After All*, 1988, after firebombing in Graz, Austria
Photo: Angelika Gradwohl

Adams specifically contributes to the legacy of his Surrealist precursors, which include postwar groups such as the Situationist International. (The Situationists, who are best remembered as the instigators of Paris '68, wanted nothing less than cultural revolution.) This legacy is very different from a Surrealism that is limited to objects preserved within the confines of a modern art museum. It respects its founding artists' vision of Surrealism as an "activity." In the twenties and thirties, the Surrealists saw their creativity as a means of transforming everyday life. They wanted to infuse pedestrian experience with the "marvelous"—what they called the surreal. This is not to say that the Surrealists and their postwar affiliates completely rejected the production of fine art; rather this was one option within a larger schema of living modern life in a creative and revitalized way. The Surrealists and their followers shared a fascination with the urban landscape: they saw the modern city as a field replete with potential chance encounters, where revelations could be triggered by stumbling upon the seemingly insignificant, marginal, and unnoticed. For them, the city was a dreamscape where one could tap one's unconscious and call forth the other within the self.

So much of Adams's work takes place on city streets—his bus shelters, his street signs, his pedestrian tunnels. He has said that his pieces, in general, are situated at "thresholds, entrances, exits," places he considers "marginal, transitional, sites that catch the viewer off guard." These marginal, "threshold" locations are appropriate sites for revealing the ellipses of collective memory, or what I've been describing as the political unconscious of a location.

Brassai, *The Statue of Marshal Ney in the Fog*, 1935

For his *Fallen Angels* project in Graz, Austria, in 1988, part of a citywide exhibition where artists were invited to create site-specific works that dealt with Graz's Nazi past, Adams chose to work on a small public-utilities pavilion across the street from an office and apartment building that had become a Hitler Youth headquarters after the German annexation of Austria in 1938. He inverted a color reproduction of the building's entrance arch, which is framed by neoclassical putti (neoclassicism was the official style of National Socialism), and within the curve of the arch, collaged right side up, he placed a black-and-white photograph of a Hitler Youth rally. He then installed this photomontage, reproduced to match the proportions of the actual building, in a light box on the pavilion. Thus, situated across the street from the site of the Nazi headquarters was a mnemonic trace documenting the building's past. Adams has emphasized the importance of this kind of displacement in his work, and the importance of the viewer, who is needed to put the pieces of the project together. At Graz, when viewers were facing the former Hitler Youth Headquarters they had to turn around to see the transposed image, whose silhouette resembles a menorah.

Adams often works with displaced elements in his pieces. This displacement is uncannily fitting for projects that deal with collective memory and the political unconscious of our social landscape. In classic Freudian analysis of the construction of memory, the mechanism of displacement is key to the functioning of memory, and it is particularly evident when we are dealing with the difficult and charged events that are most likely to be repressed and edited out of very personal reconstructions of our past.[7]

The ellipses in our collective memory reveal as much as, if not more than, what is actually remembered. The omissions, the unspoken, the disavowed represent the ideological landmarks of a population and the power–knowledge relations within a specific culture. Modernity has been obsessed with the recording of history (in a sense, history as a temporal unfolding was invented within modernity), while it has denied the historical. The razing of Wright's Imperial Hotel is representative of modernity's contradictory relationship with the past and its relentless demand for the original in fine art and the novel in popular culture. In the second half of the twentieth century, however, there has been an ever more insistent reevaluation of the historical. Since the end of World War II, modern Western culture has compulsively reexamined its history and recycled its cultural past. In the work of Dennis Adams, these recollections serve a specific and immediate purpose: they make us look at what we should not forget.

Mary Anne Staniszewski

Notes:

1. Quoted in Kathryn Smith, "Frank Lloyd Wright and the Imperial Hotel: A Postscript," *Art Bulletin*, June 1985, p. 310.

2. See Priscilla Dunhill, "Requiem for a Masterpiece," *Architectural Forum*, May 1968, pp. 70–74, and the letter from Edgar Tafel in "Letters: Tragedy of the Imperial," *Architectural Forum*, January–February 1968, p. 15.

3. All quotes from Dennis Adams are taken from a series of interviews I did with the artist during the fall of 1989.

4. The artist has acknowledged in interviews an awareness of and an interest in the analysis of the particular perspective associated with being a "stranger" or an "outsider" to issues and situations he addresses in many of his projects. In the Algerian series, Adams is an American dealing with France's relationship to its colonialist past.

   The legacy of French-Algerian conflict manifests itself today in the persistence of French racism toward the Algerians and North African immigrants. In the recent 1980s politicians like Jean-Marie Le Pen have consolidated power, and French xenophobia has become more visible. (Le Pen, who leads the ultraright National Front, won 10 percent of the votes in the 1987 French presidental election with a platform that called for expelling Arab immigrants from France.) This past year in Marseilles, for instance, Algerians have found swastikas painted on their property.

   See, for example, James M. Markham, "Marseilles Journal: If the Racism Tastes Sour, How Sweet Is Success," *New York Times*, November 16, 1988, p. A4, and "For Pieds-Noirs, the Anger Endures," *New York Times*, April 6, 1988, p. A3.

5. Duchamp's readymades challenged the modern myth of an artist's work being absolutely original. By selecting objects and calling them art, the readymade (consonant with the workings of collage, which was its exact contemporary) demonstrated that our representations and our creativity are dependent upon social codes, models exterior to the self. Just as Ferdinand de Saussure (whose lectures were given from 1906 to 1911 and were first published in 1916) argued that meaning within language has no "natural order" but is an arbitrary, cultural construct, dependent upon social conventions, the meaning and value of art, and representation in general, are not determined by natural law but are produced within a specific culture.

6. European colonial dominion expanded from about 35 percent of the earth's surface in 1815 to 85 percent by 1914. These years of what I am referring to as "high colonialism" are historically congruent with the years of high modernism, 1913 being the year Western artists achieved pure abstraction. See Edward W. Said, *Orientalism* (New York, 1978), p. 41.

7. See, for example, Sigmund Freud, "Screen Memories," in *The Complete Psychological Works of Sigmund Freud* (London, 1962), vol. 111 (1893–99).

The Algerian Annex . . . . Page 82

The Algerian Folie 86

BA(B)EL 38

Bus Shelter I 24

Bus Shelter II 26

Bus Shelter IV 66

Bus Shelter VII 44

Bus Shelter VIII 50

Bus Station 56

Fallen Angels 76

Fallingwater 34

KUNSTINSEL 78

Mass 68

Mirage 36

Patricia Hearst–A thru Z 18

Pedestrian Tunnels 74

Le Pissoir 84

A Podium for Dissent 30

Preferred Properties 42

Public Access 46

Public Commands / Other Voices 58

Reworking 60

Rudi Dutschke 70

Shifting Cinema for a Red, White, and Blue Movie 22

Street Gods / Low Rise 54

Surplus Goods / Surplus Histories 32

Ticket Booth 52

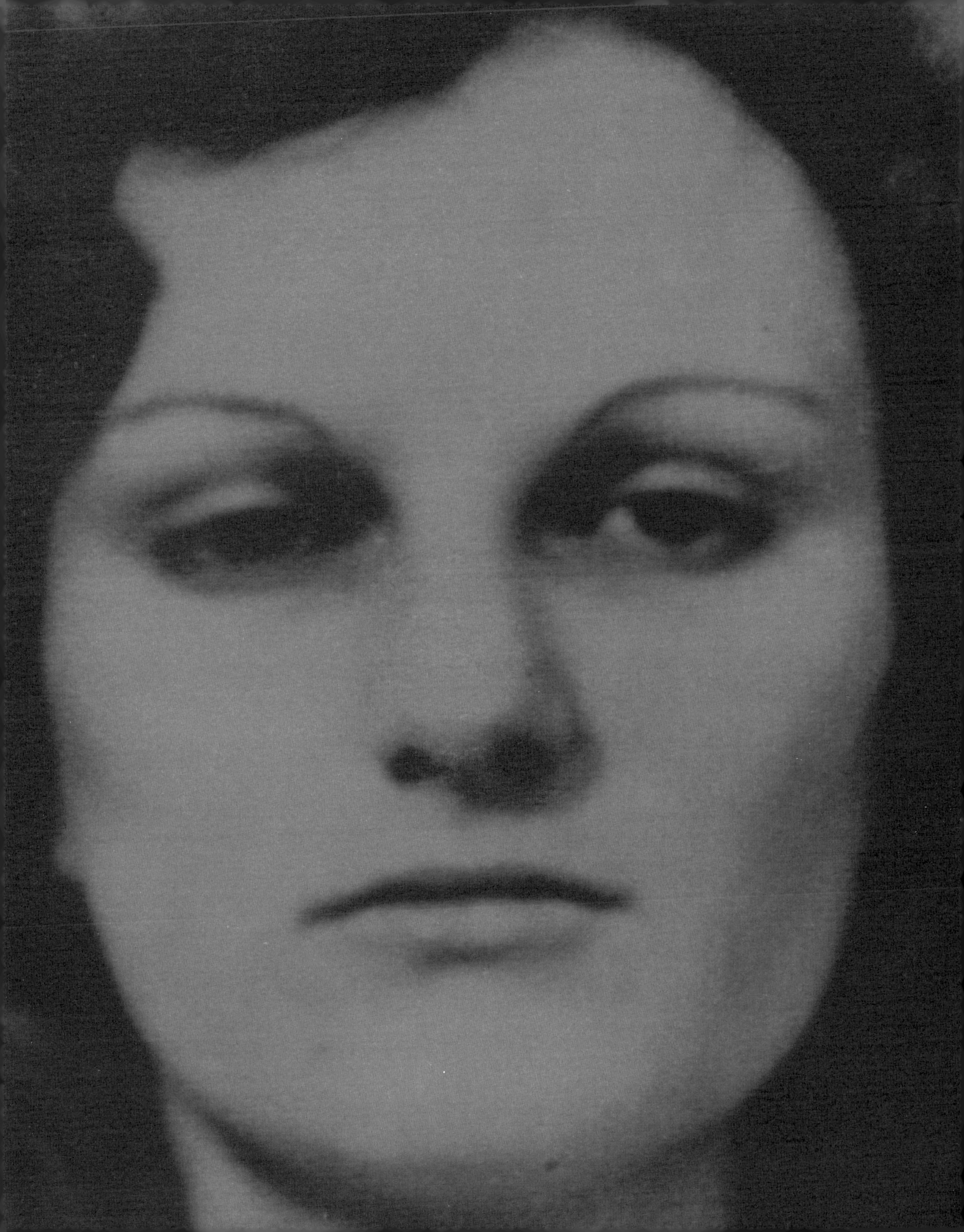

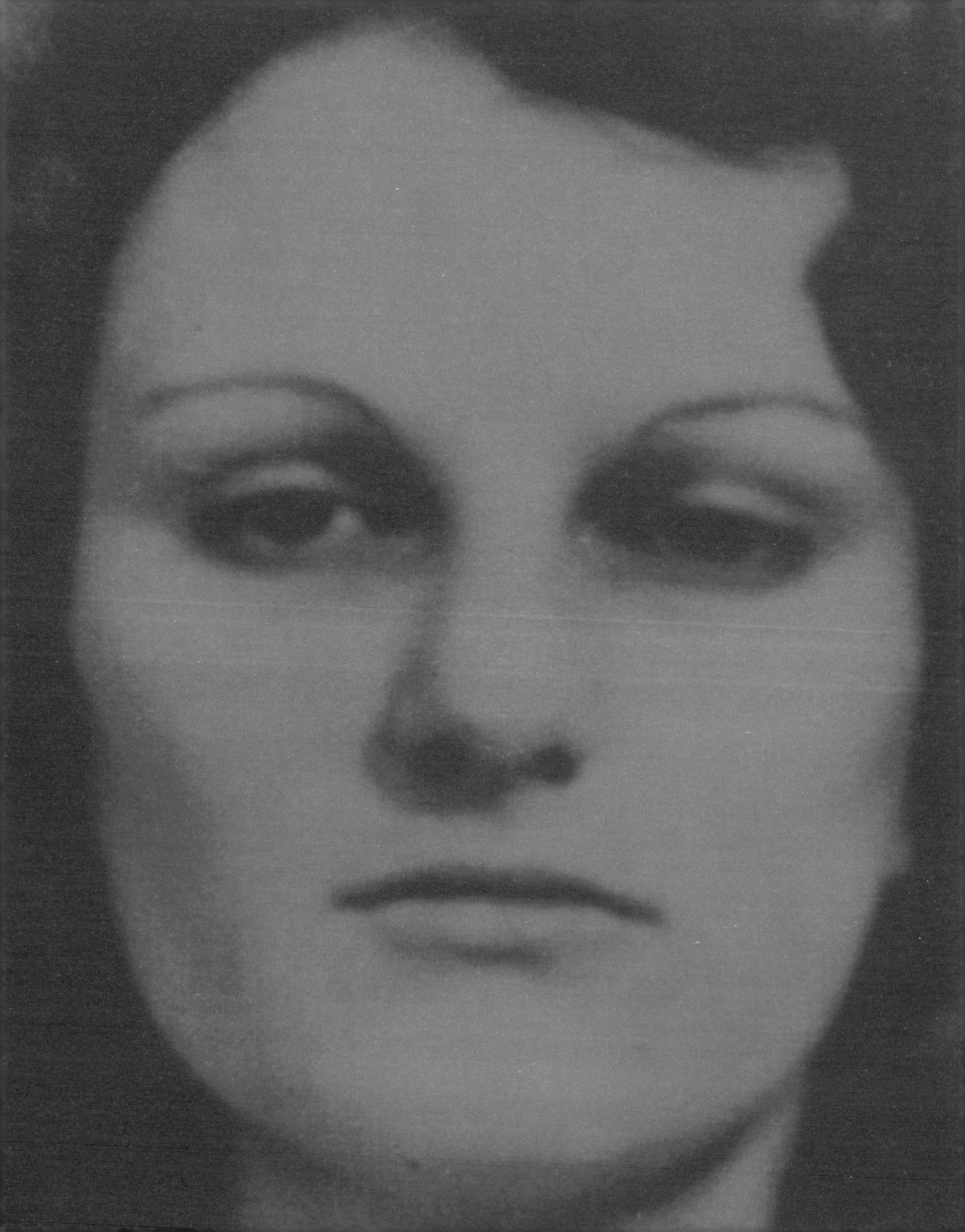

Patricia Hearst — A thru Z 1979
Minneapolis College of Art and Design

170 black-and-white photographs bracketed by two armed guards

Each photograph: 16 × 20 in. (40.6 × 50.8 cm)

Surfacing in the wake of Vietnam and Watergate, the images of Patricia Hearst circulated through our consciousness like psychological fallout, replaying America's identity crisis via the multiple and contradictory personas of a young newspaper heiress turned revolutionary terrorist. The image of Patricia Hearst—invented and reinvented by her parents, the SLA, the FBI, lawyers, and psychiatrists and then filtered through a media blitz—overloaded the circuits of representation.

For the third in a series of three exhibitions that framed the image of Patricia Hearst, I alphabetized twenty-six head shots that trace the events of her transformation, from her Communion at thirteen through her marriage to her bodyguard. These image/letter units were then combined to form twenty-six alphabetized words that were displayed across two perpendicular walls in the form of a run-on sentence that lamented the end of America. Two armed policemen were employed to stand guard, parenthetically framing the installation.

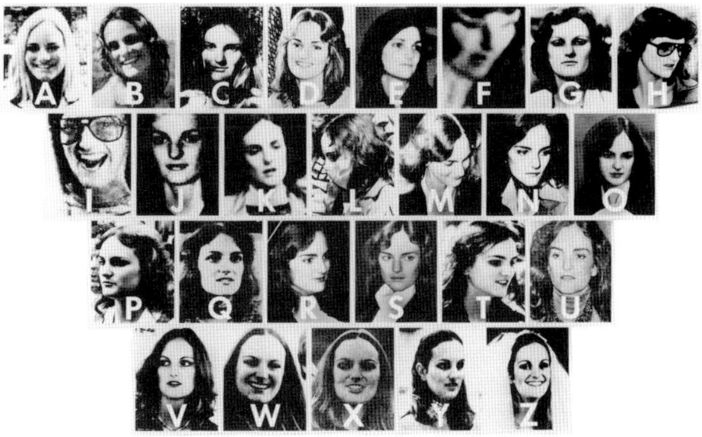

Patricia Hearst—A thru Z

Shifting Cinema for a Red, White, and Blue Movie 1980

Miami University, Oxford, Ohio

Wood and sheetrock construction painted with latex, 16 mm rear-screen projection system, and four-track sound system

108 × 564 × 492 in. (274.3 × 1432.6 × 1249.7 cm)

McCarthy holding cropped photo at Army/McCarthy Hearings

As my contribution to a three-person exhibition at Miami University entitled *Sound, Space and Performance*, I constructed an architectural installation that used found film footage and oral history to frame the rise and fall of Senator Joseph McCarthy as an anti-Communist agitator. A response to the shifting political climate of 1980 that would culminate in Ronald Reagan's victory, this installation was intended as both a memory and forecasting apparatus.

The central axis of the installation consisted of a thirty-foot wall that divided a screen for the rear projection of silent film footage from the 1954 Army/McCarthy Hearings. The division was such that two-thirds of the film frame was visible from one side and one-third from the other. This set up a primary viewing room (painted red) in which enough of the film frame was retained to recover a disparate yet narrative reading and a secondary viewing room (painted blue) that reconstituted the film frame as a fragmentary image, suggestive of low-budget pornographic films.

Maquette, 1980

To facilitate yet strategically delay passage from one room to the other, a thirty-foot corridor was constructed with a four-track sound system distributed sequentially along its length, drawing the audience through the layered anecdotes of an elderly woman who recalled her presence in 1950 at a women's club luncheon in Wheeling, West Virginia, where guest speaker Senator Joseph McCarthy first announced that he had a list of 205 Communists in the State Department.

Shifting Cinema for a Red, White, and Blue Movie

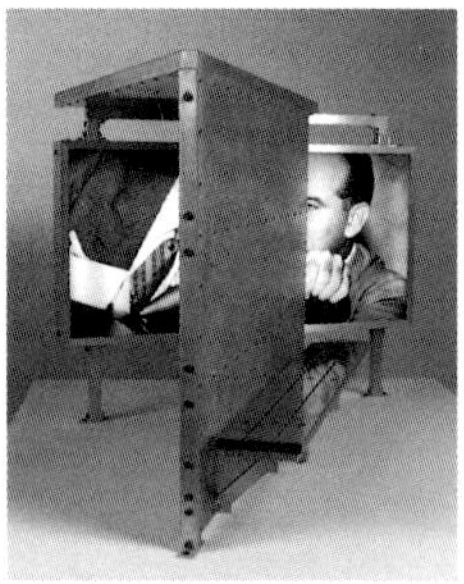

Maquette, 1981

Bus Shelter I 1983-87
Broadway and 66th Street, New York
Sponsored in part by the Public Art Fund, Inc.

Aluminum, wood, enamel, stainless steel hardware, and Duratrans between Plexiglas back-illuminated with fluorescent light

86½ × 142 × 103 in. (219.7 × 360.7 × 261.6 cm)

Constructed at street level on a bus stop at Broadway and 66th Street, *Bus Shelter I* was intended as a decoy, a mutant public amenity that would infiltrate the network of mass transit, reworking the conventional relationships between architecture, photography, and text.

The central axis of the structure consisted of a wall that separated a bench from the sheltered area that would normally be expected to contain it, as it cropped a back-illuminated photographic transparency that displayed a text on its reverse side. From 1983 to 1987 a series of photographic images and texts were filtered through the structure in disjunctive combinations that suggested multiple readings. In 1984 an image from the Army/McCarthy Hearings of Senator Joseph McCarthy and his counsel Roy Cohn was paired with a text by Jenny Holzer.

Bus Shelter 1

Maquette, 1984

Bus Shelter II 1986
14th Street and Third Avenue, New York
Sponsored in part by the Public Art Fund, Inc.

Aluminum, wood, enamel, stainless steel hardware, and Duratrans between Plexiglas back-illuminated with fluorescent light

96 × 137½ × 96½ in. (243.8 × 349.3 × 245.1 cm)

The form of *Bus Shelter II*, sited on a given bus stop at 14th Street and Third Avenue, was determined by the conceptual intersection of two bus-shelter structures, each with a bench and a double-sided, back-illuminated image/text panel. This set up a complex interface of architecture, photography, and text and paired functional elements against nonfunctional structural remnants. Inside the sheltered area, facing the oncoming buses, the two image panels each displayed a different cropped section of a photographic transparency of Ethel and Julius Rosenberg in the police truck after their arrest. On the back side of each photograph a red text was displayed against a blue ground. One panel read *Recover*, the other, *Imitations*. The words could be perceived singly, or in tandem as a command, and were intended to interact with the photographs in a disjunctive manner.

RECOVER
IMITATIONS

A Podium for Dissent 1985

Battery Park City Landfill, New York
A collaboration with Nicholas Goldsmith

Aluminum, wood, enamel, steel cables, and black-and-white photography

268 × 225 × 192 in. (680.7 × 571.5 × 487.7 cm), plus cable extensions

Sponsored by Creative Time Inc., this project was produced for the last annual *Art on the Beach* exhibition at the Battery Park City Landfill. Conceived as agitprop, the structure situated a performance stage at the intersection of the two fragments of a severed billboard-sized image of Ronald Reagan.

The completed structure was subsequently used for two performances by Ann Magnuson.

Performance by Ann Magnuson

A Podium for Dissent

Surplus Goods / Surplus Histories 1986

Formica on wood, aluminum, and Duratrans between Plexiglas back-illuminated with fluorescent light and 144 transistor radios

60 × 120 × 31 in. (152.4 × 304.8 × 78.7 cm)

Fallingwater 1988

Aluminum and Duratrans between green Plexiglas back-illuminated with fluorescent light

72 × 121½ × 38½ in (182.9 × 308.6 × 97.8 cm)

Photo: Brian Albert

Mirage 1988

Aluminum and Duratrans between Plexiglas back-illuminated with fluorescent light

41½ × 138 × 35½ in. (105.4 × 350.5 × 90.2 cm)

Photo: Lisa Kahane

BA(B)EL 1984
Maquette for an unrealized project

Plastic, aluminum, brass, enamel, and Duratrans between Plexiglas back-illuminated with fluorescent light and mounted on a wood base

110¾ × 14¼ × 18 in. (281.3 × 36.2 × 45.7 cm)

BA(B)EL is a maquette for an unrealized speaker's lectern. It elevates the utopian legacy of Constructivism only to demonstrate its ultimate collapse, framing the historical tragedy of Modernism.

The proposed height of the completed tower is forty-four feet four inches. Five back-illuminated image panels are suspended through its central axis. The back side of the center panel, the only level plane in the entire structure, functions as the speaker's podium.

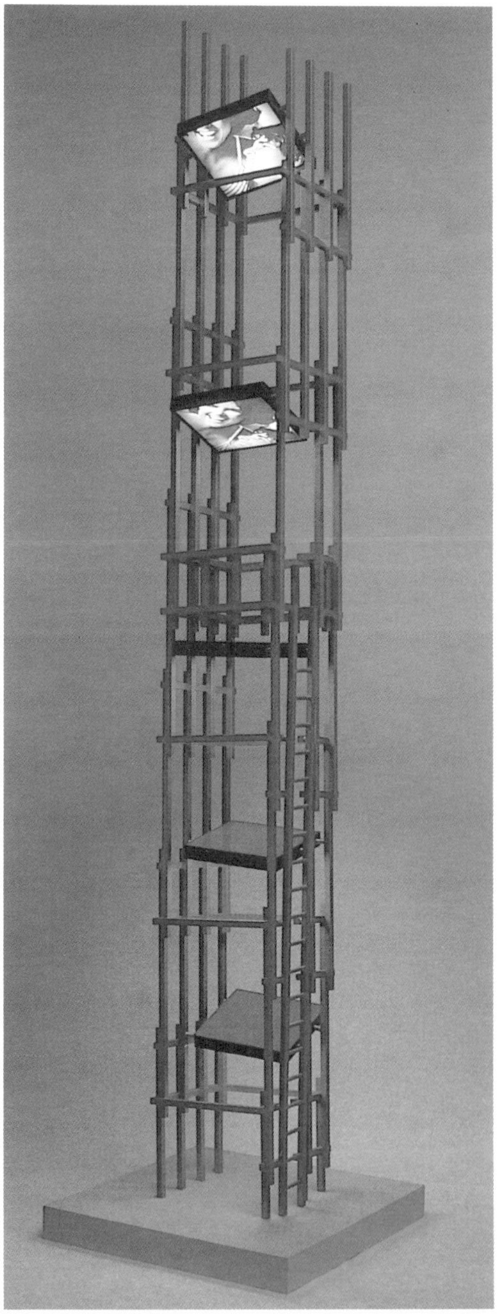

BA(B)EL

Preferred Properties 1989

Aluminum, steel hardware, and Duratrans between Plexiglas back-illuminated with fluorescent light.

Easel structure: 132 × 88½ × 54½ in. (335.3 × 224.8 × 138.4 cm). Inset photographic transparency: 20 × 24 in. (50.8 × 61 cm)

Preferred Properties was conceived as an excessive structural scaffolding for the display of a back-illuminated photographic transparency of the American Embassy in Saigon. The easel was constructed inside out, so that the photographic transparency was captured in the structural network of the architecture. On the opposite side of the gallery, facing the easel, a smaller and differently cropped version of the same photograph was installed flush with the wall.

Photos: Fred Scruten

Student demonstration during the 1968 Chicago Democratic Convention

Bus Shelter VII 1988
Long Island University, Brookville, New York

Outside: Duratrans between Plexiglas back-illuminated with fluorescent light in an aluminum display case mounted between two existing bus shelters.
Inside: street lamp on a wood base between two black-and-white photographs

Display case: 96½ × 21¾ × 6 in. (245.1 × 55.2 × 15.2 cm). Each black-and-white photograph: 30 × 8 in. (76.2 × 20.3 cm)

For a six-person exhibition entitled *Insight/On Site* at C. W. Post Campus of Long Island University, each artist was asked to produce a temporary outdoor project and to exhibit the working artifacts of its conceptualization inside the university's art gallery.

For my project, I removed a street lamp that was situated between two adjacent shelter structures at a bus stop servicing the campus and reinstalled it in the university's art gallery. In its place, I installed a fluorescent-illuminated sign that joined the two shelters and displayed a translucent photographic image of a student demonstration during the 1968 Chicago Democratic Convention. This image was extracted from the center section of a larger photograph, the two end fragments of which were then installed inside the campus gallery, parenthetically framing the street lamp.

Site before installation

Photo: Tom Brokish

Photo: Tom Brokish

Public Access 1989

Galerie Meert-Rihoux, Brussels

Steel fencing, Plexiglas backboard with steel basketball hoop, two Cibachrome translucent prints between Plexiglas back-illuminated with fluorescent light in two aluminum display cases

Interior steel fencing: 135 × 196¾ × 4 in.
(343 × 500 × 10 cm)
Each display case: 47¼ × 70¾ × 5½ in.
(120 × 180 × 14 cm)

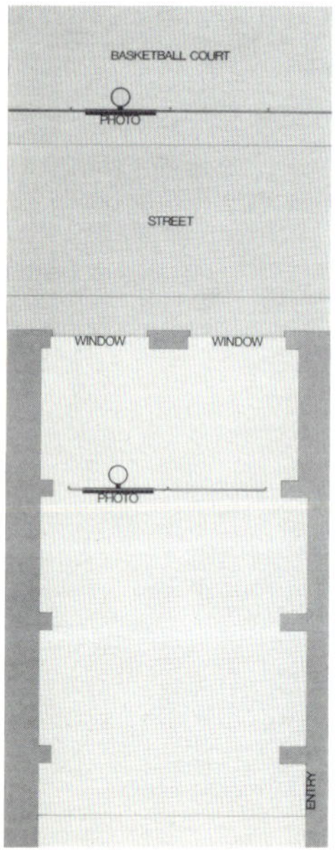

Installation Plan

The privileged image of the Galerie Meert-Rihoux is in stark contrast to the immigrant working class neighborhood that surrounds it. This difference is mediated by two large windows at the front of the exhibition space that theatrically frame a street-level view of a basketball court that is frequented by Algerian, Moroccan, Tunisian, and Turkish youths.

Inside the gallery I reconstructed a cross section of the steel fencing that encloses the basketball court and one of the backboard/hoop units it supports. Placed on a parallel axis to its outdoor prototype and facing the street, this structure reframed the window view as it divided the exhibition area into two distinct spaces. On the reverse side of the reconstructed backboard/hoop, facing the gallery entrance, I suspended a back-illuminated photograph of a large group of immigrant Turkish males crowding the foreground in front of a police barricade. A detail of this photograph was then mounted in an identical back-illuminated display case on the reverse side of the outdoor backboard/hoop unit. The completed installation functioned as a layering between inside and out—a social index at the edge of gentrification.

Photos: Fabien de Cugnac

Bus Shelter VIII 1988
Queen and Bay Streets, Toronto
Sponsored by Cold City Gallery

Aluminum, smoked and clear high-tempered glass, galvanized steel hardware, and Duratrans under glass back-illuminated with fluorescent light

Each bus shelter: 86 × 144 × 53 in.
(218.4 × 365.8 × 134.6 cm)

On a traffic island at one of the busiest intersections in Toronto and across the street from City Hall, I constructed two conventional-looking bus shelters at an oblique angle to one another. The shelter that faced the oncoming buses functioned like a standard glass-enclosed waiting space with a bench inside. Running the length of its back side and facing the other shelter was a light box displaying a photographic image of native Canadian Indians staging a street protest outside the Parliament building in Ottawa. As dusk came on, this photographic image reflected off and through the second shelter, which was made of smoked glass and was completely enclosed, without an entrance. Barred from its functional program and operating only as a receiving zone for the photographic image, the second shelter became a kind of phantasmagorical replica of the first. The plight of the dispossessed reverberated through the structural interfacing of two architectural bodies.

Maquette 1988, Photo: Ali Elai

Photo: Lenscape Incorporated

Ticket Booth 1989
Whitney Museum of American Art, New York

Formica and aluminum laminas on wood, and Duratrans between Plexiglas back-illuminated with fluorescent light

67½ × 138 × 97 in. (171.5 × 350.5 × 246.4 cm)

This project was produced for *Image World*, a large group exhibition that surveyed the influence of mass media and image-making technologies on American art from Warhol to the present.

Working outside the immediate context of the exhibition, I produced a functioning ticket booth that was used for general admission in the museum's entrance lobby. The facade of the structure consisted of an exchange window that penetrated a back-illuminated photographic transparency of two homeless men vending on the streets of New York City. This facade was then duplicated as a nonfunctional dummy that enclosed the back side of the booth framing the ticket vendor.

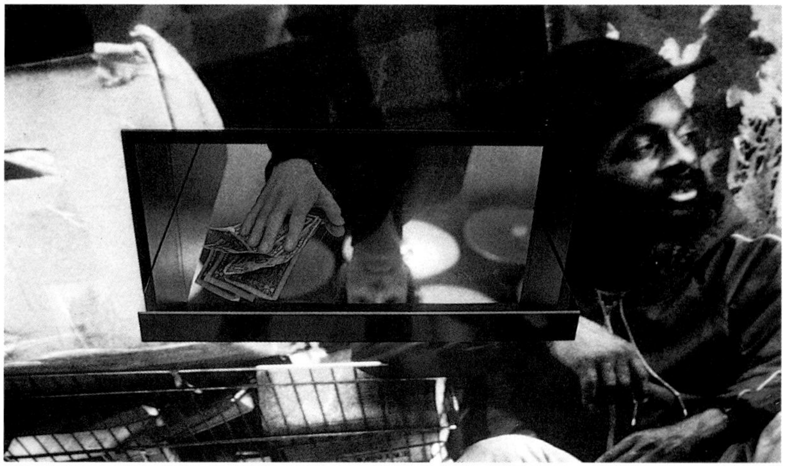

Detail Photo: Victor Bouillon

Photo: Ali Elai

Street Gods / Low Rise 1988
The Clocktower, New York

Wood platform illuminated from below with fluorescent light, eight Duratrans between Plexiglas back-illuminated with fluorescent light

Given room: 252 × 372 × 372 in.
(640.1 × 944.9 × 944.9 cm)

During the 1987–88 season the Clocktower organized a series of four consecutive exhibitions that traced developments in Pop Art from the Independent Group to the present. For one exhibition in this series, Krzysztof Wodiczko and I produced separate installations that confronted the issue of urban homelessness.

For my part, I addressed the verticality of the upper-level exhibition space of the Clocktower, with its twenty-one-foot ceilings and spiral staircase, as an urban metaphor of social exclusion. In the center of the space a platform was constructed that rotated off the given axis of the room and was illuminated from below by four banks of fluorescent lights. Its elevation was determined by extending the first step of the spiral staircase. The four windows that frame the upper portion of the room and punctuate the symmetry of the space were filled in with back-illuminated photographic transparencies of four homeless New Yorkers. Taken from a low vantage point so that each figure's gaze was directed downward toward the platform, the photographs inverted the classical alignment of power. As a final gesture, a second set of four duplicate back-illuminated photographic transparencies were installed upside down directly above the first set, so that they were cropped by the intersection of the ceiling. This destabilized the vertical boundaries of the architecture, suggesting the continuation of the images.

Photo: Peter Bellamy

Photo: Peter Bellamy

Bus Station 1988

West and Liberty Streets, New York
A collaboration with Andrea Blum

Duratrans between Lexan back-illuminated with fluorescent light in an aluminum display case that intersects a cast-concrete bench

47 × 300 × 96 in. (119.4 × 762 × 243.8 cm)

This project was produced for an exhibition entitled *The New Urban Landscape*. A group of thirty-two artists and architects were asked to make temporary installations to inaugurate the opening of the public spaces in the World Financial Center, the centerpiece of the Battery Park City Development in lower Manhattan.

To avoid the homogenized atmosphere of the site and not wanting our work to be contextualized as another corporate trophy, Andrea Blum and I decided to move outside the Battery Park City property line onto West Street, which defines the development's eastern boundary. Conceived as a waiting station, our piece was sited on an existing bus stop that services the airport. The structure was built long and low to the ground, countering the overwhelming scale of the surrounding buildings as they project an image of corporate power and suggesting a kind of tentacle of investment. It consisted of a twenty-five-foot-long concrete bench intersected by a light box that projected out of the ground and displayed a photographic transparency of a funeral procession in Soweto, South Africa.

Bus Station

Public Commands / Other Voices 1988
Martin Luther King, Jr. Metrorail Station, Miami

Thirty Type-C prints mounted over the existing speakers of the Metrorail public address system

Each print: 30 × 40 in. (76.2 × 101.6 cm)

In conjunction with the New Music America-Miami Festival, six artists were invited to the city to produce temporary sound installations at six different Metrorail stations.

I was asked to work at the Martin Luther King, Jr. Station, which services an African-American neighborhood. For my installation, I framed the thirty ceiling speakers of the public address system that runs the length of both sides of the station with photographs of American black civil rights activists delivering speeches. My intention was to confront the visual anonymity of this system as it confirms the entrenched power of public authority, and to revive historical voices of dissent as a kind of prescription for talking back.

"men at work" barricade in Geneva

Reworking 1988
Geneva

Thirty-six black-and-white photographs mounted on aluminum and sealed with plastic laminate, each attached to a barricade of wood, steel stanchions, and cinder block

Each barricade: 159¾ × 33½ × 45 in. (406 × 85 × 114 cm)

At the base of Geneva's thriving economy is a large immigrant work force drawn principally from southern Europe and northern Africa. As part of a group exhibition entitled *Reprises de vues* sponsored by Halle Sud in Geneva, I produced a series of public interventions that identified this underground community.

Thirty-six permutations of the standard "men at work" barricades that partition off the city's construction sites were fabricated. The triangular signs that conventionally punctuate these barricades, framing a graphic logo of an anonymous figure at work, were inverted, hung at eye level, and each covered with a photographic head shot of an immigrant worker. The name of each worker's native village was then stenciled repeatedly along the vertical axis of the corresponding barricade, where the sponsoring construction company would normally place its trade name.

These thirty-six altered barricades were then situated in various combinations and configurations on eighteen public sites as indexes to Geneva's economic subtext, framing the parks, monuments, and institutions that perpetuate the city's liberal/humanist image.

SENTRE TETES
ANNEMASSE
REGGIO EMILIA
ZAGHOUAN

Chancy
Jonction
Annecy
Lyon
P Plainpalais
Lausanne
AÉROPORT

PATRIE
1914 1918

Maquette, 1987

Bus Shelter IV 1987

Domplatz, Münster, West Germany

Aluminum, Plexiglas, wood, enamel, stainless steel hardware, and Duratrans between Plexiglas back-illuminated with fluorescent light

120 × 201 × 156 in. (304.8 × 510.5 × 396.2 cm)

Bus Shelter IV was produced for *Skulptur Projekte in Münster*, a large international exhibition of temporary outdoor public projects.

Sited on the Domplatz at a given bus stop at the center of the city, the structure of the shelter was divided into two seating areas that were bracketed by double-sided, back-illuminated image panels. Except for a roof that covered the bench facing the street and an image panel that extended up through it, one seating area was a mirror image of the other. The sides of the two image panels that faced out displayed duplicate photographs of the Klaus Barbie trial that was in progress at the time of the installation. Jacques Verges, Barbie's lawyer, is in the foreground, and behind him Klaus Barbie sits in the defendant's box. The insides of the two panels each displayed a duplicate blown-up image of an anonymous man excerpted from the background of the trial scene on the reverse side.

Detail

Bus Shelter IV

Mass 1988

Aluminum and Duratrans between Plexiglas back-illuminated with fluorescent light

82¾ × 68 × 60¼ in. (210 × 172.7 × 15.3 cm)

Rudi Dutschke 1989

Black and white photograph mounted on aluminum and stainless steel case displaying Cibachrome translucent print between Plexiglas back-illuminated with fluorescent light

82¾ × 68 × 60¼ in. (180 × 64 × 135 cm)

Photo: Hanns Joosten

Pedestrian Tunnels 1989

Esslingen, West Germany

Twelve Cibachrome translucent prints between Plexiglas back-illuminated with fluorescent light in six two-way aluminum display cases

Each display case: 15¾ × 93½ × 6½ in.
(40 × 237.5 × 16.5 cm)

For the first *Internationale Foto-Triennale*, held in Esslingen in 1989, I reissued the directional signs that guide the public through three pedestrian tunnels that pass underneath a highway that cuts through the city. The existing sign that was suspended from the entrance and exit of each tunnel was removed and replaced with a two-way light box. On the side facing out, the names of the street destinations were reissued in their original orientation, in a black Fractura typeface on a red ground—a style and color associated with the Nazi period. On the other sides of the light boxes, facing into the tunnels, was a series of six photographic transparencies, extracted from images of Nazi rituals, that documented fragmented bodies in motion.

Fallen Angels 1988
Graz, Austria

Duratrans between Plexiglas back-illuminated with fluorescent light in a steel display case mounted on an existing public electrical pavilion

Display case: 82 × 152¾ × 6¼ in. (208 × 388 × 16 cm)

As the premise for an exhibition entitled *Points of Reference 38/88* sponsored by an annual cultural festival known as the Styrian Autumn, sixteen artists were invited to Graz, the capital of the Austrian providence of Styria, to produce temporary public installations on preselected sites that the curator, Dr. Werner Fenz, and his staff had identified as strongholds of Nazi indoctrination after the German annexation of Austria in 1938.

For my installation, I addressed the existing entrance of the building that formerly housed the Hitler Youth Headquarters and today functions as offices and apartments. The arched window above the doorway, which is flanked by a pair of putti, was photographically reconstructed. The photograph was inverted, and the glass panes of the window were covered with a collaged photograph of a Hitler Youth rally. This altered image was then reproduced on translucent film in a scale equivalent to the measurements of the existing architecture and installed in a light box that was strategically situated on a public electrical pavilion in a small park that overlooks the building's entrance.

Hitler Youth Headquarters, Graz 1938

Photo: Dietmar Tanterl

KUNSTINSEL 1989
Hamburg

Steel and wood scaffolding set in a concrete foundation, black-and-white photography mounted on Plexiglas, and incandescent floodlights

354¼ × 196¾ × 59 in. (900 × 500 × 150 cm)

This project was produced in conjunction with a large international exhibition entitled *D & S Ausstellung* that was sponsored by the Kunstverein in Hamburg. In addition to several public sites, the principal exhibition was held in the Kunstverein and the Kunsthaus, both of which are scheduled for demolition in 1990 to make way for O. M. Ungers's new museum/plaza complex, Kunstinsel.

On the very edge of the museum's property line, I ordered the construction of a large billboard in the style associated with the promotion of projected building sites. Displayed on the billboard above the word KUNSTINSEL is a staged photograph that shows two traditional Turkish immigrant women conversing over Ungers's maquette for the proposed museum/plaza complex. (As members of a disenfranchised community in West Germany, Turks would not normally be represented as a part of any promotional advertising, or in any scenario that suggested their participation in public discussion.)

The project will remain in place through the construction phase of the complex.

Photo: Wolfgang Neeb

KUNSTINSEL
P

The Algerian Annex 1989

Musée d'Art Moderne de la Ville de Paris

Wood construction, four slide-projection systems, four postwar abstract paintings from the museum's permanent collection, and mirrored floor panels

Altered room: 113½ × 485½ × 245 in. (288 × 1233 × 620 cm)

This installation was produced for a four-person exhibition entitled *Images Critiques* at the Musée d'Art Moderne de la Ville de Paris. The exhibition room I chose for my installation is in itself a very strong image. Bracketed by the entrance and exit stairs and enclosed by a glass facade, it feels like a vacuum at the center of the museum. In response, I addressed its architecture as a kind of matrix for the museum context at large, confronting its authority as the archive of official history. Four postwar abstract paintings were removed from the museum's permanent collection and reinstalled inside this room on a constructed wall that was suspended above the floor at knee level. A panoramic image of Algerian women and children charging the camera during a 1962 street demonstration for Algerian independence was then projected from behind the wall in such a way that it reflected down into a mirrored floor that was installed throughout the room.

Detail of suspended wall with painting by Hans Hartung above reflected image of a street demonstration for Algerian independence. Photos: Quentin Bertoux

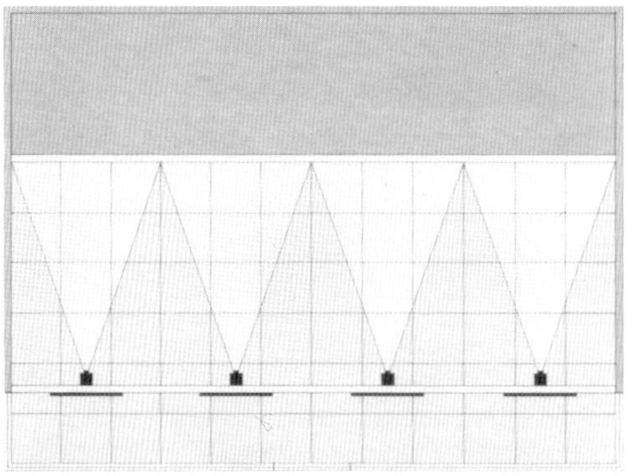

Installation plan of paintings in relation to the projection system. Grid represents mirrored floor panels.

The Algerian Annex

Le Pissoir 1988

Maquette for Dijon, France

Plexiglas spray-painted with lacquer, Duratrans between Plexiglas back-illuminated with fluorescent light and mounted on a wood base

17½ × 33¼ × 12¼ in. (44.5 × 84.5 × 31.1 cm)

This project was initiated by the Consortium for Dijon. Its proposed material, structure and scale were based on the city's old public pissoirs. Made of cast concrete, these bunkerlike pavilions house two urinal chambers that each conform to the proportions of the human body. The displaced look of these worn, urban remnants against the background of the developing city suggested the appropriation of their form as an image of collective memory, and as a potential vessel for the distribution of historical photographs.

Specifically, I proposed to construct a schematic replica of a pissoir's exterior shell and inside, in place of the urinal niches, to display two identical back-illuminated photographic transparencies. Taken in 1962, these images show the dismantled statuary of French military governors lying in the sand, awaiting shipment back to France during the closing moments of Algeria's War of Independence. The pavilion was proposed for the entrance of the boulevard Charles de Gaulle.

Because of the controversial form and subject of this project, it has not yet been realized. It exists only in maquette form. It was first exhibited in April 1989 at Christine Burgin Gallery in New York, behind a wall housing a life-sized, back-illuminated photograph of one of Dijon's existing pissoirs.

Installation view, Christine Burgin Gallery, 1989. Photos: Ken Showell

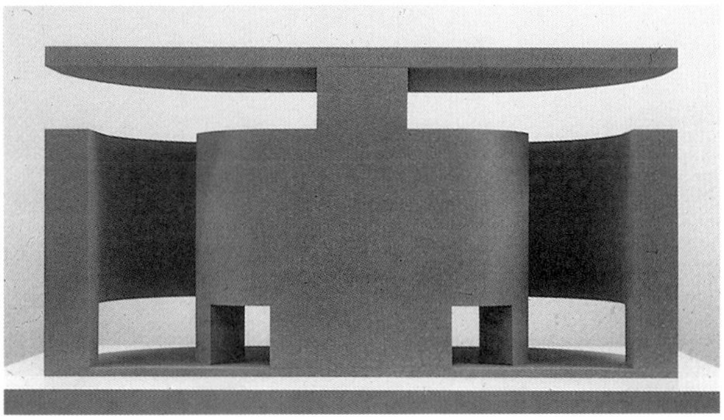

The Algerian Folie 1989
Parc La Villette, Paris

Flatbed truck trailer interfaced with two aluminum cases, each displaying Cibachrome translucent prints between Plexiglas back-illuminated with fluorescent light. All metal surfaces painted in red enamel

134 × 94½ × 413½ in. (340 × 240 × 1050 cm)

This installation was produced for an exhibition entitled *Magiciens de la Terre* that was organized by the Centre Georges Pompidou in Paris and held simultaneously at the Musée National d'Art Moderne and the Grande Halle at Parc La Villette. The exhibition was proposed as the first comprehensive international exhibition of artists from the so-called First and Third Worlds.

I chose to place my work directly outside the entrance of the Grande Halle at Parc La Villette, as a critical prologue to the potential colonialist image of the exhibition. At the time of the exhibition, the surrounding park was under construction with Bernard Tschumi's architectural Folies. I appropriated one of the flatbed truck trailers that were part of the visual vernacular of the building sites, bracketing the length of its structure with two back-illuminated photographic transparencies of the dismantled statuary of French military governors lying in the sand, awaiting shipment back to France during the closing moments of Algeria's War of Independence.

***Exile* I** *1989.*
30 × 81 × 18 in. (76 × 206 × 46 cm)
Wood, aluminum and Duratrans between Plexiglas back-illuminated with flourescent light.
Photo: Fabien de Cugnac

BIOGRAPHY

Born 1948, Des Moines, Iowa

Public Works

1978 *Patricia Hearst—A Second Reading*. 10 on 8, New York
1983 *Bus Shelter I*. Broadway and 66th Street, New York
1985 *A Podium for Dissent*. Battery Park City Landfill, New York. In collaboration with Nicholas Goldsmith and Ann Magnuson
1986 *Bus Shelter II*. 14th Street and 3rd Avenue, New York
1987 *Bus Shelter IV*. Domplatz, Münster, West Germany
1988 *Bus Shelter VII*. C. W. Post Campus of Long Island University, Brookville, New York
Reworking. Geneva
Fallen Angels. Graz, Austria
Public Commands/Other Voices. Martin Luther King Jr. Metrorail Station, Miami, Florida
Bus Station. West and Liberty Streets, New York. In collaboration with Andrea Blum
Bus Shelter VIII. Queen and Bay Streets, Toronto
1989 *Ticket Booth*. Whitney Museum of American Art, New York
Pedestrian Tunnels. Esslingen, West Germany
KUNSTINSEL. Hamburg
The Procession. La Grande Arche, La Défense, Paris

Solo Exhibitions / Installations

1971 Philadelphia Art Alliance
1972 Akron Art Institute, Akron, Ohio
1974 Carl Solway Gallery, Cincinnati, Ohio
1975 Wright State University, Dayton, Ohio
Carl Solway Gallery, Cincinnati, Ohio
1976 Tyler School of Art, Philadelphia
1978 D.C. Space, Washington, D.C.
1979 Artists Space, New York
Minneapolis College of Art and Design, Minneapolis, Minnesota
1980 California State University, Long Beach, California
Miami University, Oxford, Ohio
1984 The Kitchen, New York
1985 East Carolina University, Greenville, North Carolina
1986 Nature Morte Gallery, New York
1987 Alternative Museum, New York
City University Graduate Center Mall, New York
1988 The Clocktower, New York
Galerie Gabrielle Maubrie, Paris
Nature Morte Gallery, New York
de Appel Foundation, Amsterdam
Cleveland State University, Cleveland, Ohio
1989 John Weber Gallery, New York
Galerie Meert-Rihoux, Brussels
Christine Burgin Gallery, New York

Selected Group Exhibitions

1974 *American Painting and Sculpture Today*. Contemporary Arts Center, Cincinnati, Ohio
1977 *Contemporary Drawing Invitational*. Lake Placid School of Art, Lake Placid, New York
Art Stories. Libra Gallery, Claremont Graduate School, Claremont, California
Allegoria dell'impronta digitale. Galleria Mercato Del Sale, Milan
Great Enlargements. Midway Studios, Chicago
1978 *Artwords and Bookworks*. Los Angeles Institute of Contemporary Art
1979 *In the Shadow of Marcel Duchamp*. Grolier Club and Franklin Furnace, New York
Reality of Illusion. Denver Art Museum, Denver, Colorado; University of Southern California at Los Angeles; Honolulu Academy of the Arts, Honolulu, Hawaii; Cornell University, Ithaca, New York; Oakland Museum, Oakland, California; Toledo Museum, Toledo, Ohio; University of Texas, Austin, Texas
1980 *Sound, Space and Performance*. Miami University, Oxford, Ohio
1981 *Libres d'artista/Artists' Books*. Metronom, Barcelona
1982 *100 Anniversary Invitational Art Exhibition*. YM/YWHA, Union, New Jersey
1983 *The Ponderosa Collection*. Butler Institute of American Art, Youngstown, Ohio
Grab Bag. City Gallery, New York
Subculture. Organized by Group Material. IRT subway trains, New York; C.E.P.A., Buffalo, New York
Persuasion(s). The Kitchen, New York
1984 *Hundreds of Drawings*. Artists Space, New York
Metamanhattan. Whitney Museum of American Art Downtown, New York
Site Specific Proposals. East Carolina University, Greenville, North Carolina
Contemporary Perspectives 1984. Center Gallery, Bucknell University, Lewisburg, Pennsylvania; Sordoni Art Gallery, Wilkes College, Wilkes-Barre, Pennsylvania
1985 *Not Just Any Pretty Picture*. Part of the multigallery project State of Union/State of Mind. P.S. 122, New York
The Artist as Social Designer: Aspects of Urban Art Today. Los Angeles Museum of Art
Disinformation: The Manufacture of Consent. Alternative Museum, New York
Mass. Organized by Group Material. Hallwalls, Buffalo, New York; Spaces, Cleveland, Ohio; Arts Consortium, Cincinnati, Ohio; Aljira Arts, Newark, New Jersey; New Museum of Contemporary Art, New York
Art on the Beach. Battery Park City Landfill, New York
1986 *Homeless at Home*. Storefront for Art and Architecture, New York
Liberty and Justice. Alternative Museum, New York
Cinemaobject. City Gallery, New York
Lost/Found Language. Lawrence Gallery, Rosemont College, Rosemont, Pennsylvania
Uplifted Atmospheres, Borrowed Taste. Hallwalls, Buffalo, New York
The Homecoming. University of Northern Iowa, Cedar Falls, Iowa. Traveled to five Iowa museums
1987 *Spectre of Saturation*. McIntosh/Drysdale Gallery, Washington, D.C.
Im Auftrag. Museum Folkwang, Essen, West Germany
Atlantic Sculpture. Art Center College of Design, Pasadena, California
Dennis Adams, Tony Brown, Dan Graham, Rodney Graham. de Appel Foundation, Amsterdam
Skulptur Projekte in Münster 1987. Westfälisches Landesmuseum, Münster, West Germany
Art in the Dark. City Without Walls, Newark, New Jersey
Constitution. Organized by Group Material. Temple Gallery, Temple University, Philadelphia
Nightfire. de Appel Foundation, Amsterdam
New York Art. Ace Contemporary Exhibitions, Los Angeles

1988 *Constructions: Between Sculpture and Architecture.* Sculpture Center, New York
Material Ethics. Milford Gallery, New York
Photography on the Edge. Haggerty Museum of Art, Marquette University, Milwaukee, Wisconsin
Insight/On Site. Hillwood Art Gallery, C. W. Post Campus of Long Island University, Brookville, New York
Presi x incantamento: La nuova fotografia internazionale. Padiglione d'Arte Contemporanea, Milan
Reprises de vues. Halle Sud, Geneva
Accrochage 1: Dennis Adams, Dan Graham, Louise Lawler. Galerie Meert-Rihoux, Brussels
Rendez-vous manqués. Galerie Gabrielle Maubrie, Paris
L'inventaire/Les dimensions ordinaires. Manufrance, Saint-Etienne, France
The Whole World Is Still Watching. Randolph Street Gallery, Chicago
The Plight of the Figure. Islip Art Museum, East Islip, New York
Politically Charged. First Street Forum, Saint Louis, Missouri
Bezugspunkte 38/88. Steirischer Herbst, Graz, Austria
Dennis Adams, Alfredo Jaar, Jeff Wall. Tomoko Liguori Gallery, New York
New Music America-Miami Festival. Miami, Florida
Public Discourse. Real Artways, Hartford, Connecticut
Unknown Secrets: Art and the Rosenberg Era. Organized by the Rosenberg Era Art Project. Hillwood Art Gallery, C. W. Post Campus of Long Island University, Brookville, New York; Massachusetts College of Art North Gallery, Boston; Olin Gallery, Kenyon College, Gambier, Ohio; Palmer Museum of Art, Pennsylvania State University, University Park, Pennsylvania; University of Colorado Art Gallery, Boulder, Colorado; San Diego State University Art Gallery, San Diego, California; Otis Art Institute of Parsons School of Design Gallery, Los Angeles; San Francisco Jewish Community Museum; Spertus Museum of Judaica, Chicago; Brody Gallery and Addison-Ripley Gallery, Washington, D.C.
The New Urban Landscape. World Financial Center, New York
Publics Art: Dennis Adams, Alan Belcher. Cold City Gallery, Toronto
Dennis Adams, Christian Boltanski, Sophie Calle, Alfredo Jaar, Stephen Laub, Antonio Muntadas. Craig Cornelius Gallery, New York

1989 *Images Critiques: Adams, Jaar, Jammes, Wall.* L'ARC, Musée d'Art Moderne de la Ville de Paris
Conspicuous Display. Stedman Art Gallery, Rutgers University, Camden, New Jersey
Sequence (Con)Sequence: (Sub)Versions of Photography in the 80s. Edith C. Blum Art Institute, Bard College, Annandale-on-Hudson, New York
Fonds National d'Art Contemporain: Acquisitions 1988. Fondation Nationale des Arts Graphiques et Plastiques, Paris
Revamp, Review. Center for Photography at Woodstock, Woodstock, New York
The Photography of Invention: American Pictures of the 1980s. National Museum of American Art, Smithsonian Institution, Washington, D.C.; Museum of Contemporary Art, Chicago; Walker Art Center, Minneapolis, Minnesota
Jet Lag. Turon Travel, New York
Bientôt 3 ans. Galerie Gabrielle Maubrie, Paris
Magiciens de la Terre. Musée National d'Art Moderne, Centre Georges Pompidou, and La Grande Halle, Parc La Villette, Paris
Dennis Adams, Alan Belcher, Jennifer Bolande. Margo Leavin Gallery, Los Angeles
Public Domain. Kent Fine Art, New York
Tenir l'image à distance. Musée d'Art Contemporain, Montreal
Not Photography. Meyers Bloom Gallery, Santa Monica, California
D & S Ausstellung. Kunstverein Hamburg
Strategie & Rhetorik: Dennis Adams, John Baldessari, Jochen Gerz. Galerie Anselm Dreher, West Berlin
1. Internationale Foto-Triennale. Villa Merkel, Esslingen, West Germany
Dennis Adams, Christian Boltanski, Alfredo Jaar. Elwood Fine Arts, Seattle, Washington
Dennis Adams, Ange Leccia, Not Vital. Galerie Faust, Geneva
FAUXtography. Art Center College of Design, Pasadena, California
Image World: Art and Media Culture. Whitney Museum of American Art, New York
Outdoor Projects: Dan Graham, Dennis Adams, Ludger Gerdes. Ulla Klot, Hamburg

Selected Bibliography

1972 Carr, Carolyn. "Fascination in Show: Art Is Nature Is Art." *Akron Beacon Journal*, March 12, p. D9.

1973 Donohoe, Victoria. "Do-It-Yourselfers Prevail at New Gallery." *Philadelphia Inquirer*, June 15, p. 2C.
McCaslin, Walt. "Not in N.Y. Gallery." *Dayton Journal Herald*, November 5, p. 23.

1974 Brown, Ellen. "Scientific Approach to Art." *Cincinnati Post*, April 6, p. 22.
Findsen, Owen. "Science Secrets." *Cincinnati Enquirer*, April 7, p. 6F.

1975 Brown, Ellen. "Dennis Adams: Finding the Common Denominator." *Cincinnati Post*, May 3, p. 22.
Findsen, Owen. "Visual Words and Music." *Cincinnati Enquirer*, May 11, p. 6F.

1976 *Spawn Press Editions* (Akron, Ohio), March.

1977 Pelta, Maureen. "Finnegan's Wake: A Second Reading." *Philadelphia Arts Exchange*, January–February, p. 37.
Muchnic, Suzanne. "Artists' Books." *Artweek*, February 26, pp. 1, 16.
Adams, Dennis. *Behind Social Studies.* New York: self-published.

1978 Waggoner, Walter H. "Artist Protests City's Removing Miss Hearst Show." *New York Times*, November 19, sec. 1, p. 64.
Marzorati, Gerald. "Hearst Heist." *Soho Weekly News*, November 23, p. 11.
Glueck, Grace. "Art People." *New York Times*, November 24, p. C21.
Brill, Rob. "Too Hot for Hearst to Handle." *Village Voice*, November 27, p. 102.

1979 Hegman, William R. "Looking at Art." *Minneapolis Tribune*, September 30.
Patricia Hearst—A thru Z. Exhibition brochure, Minneapolis College of Art and Design, Minneapolis, Minnesota. Introduction by John Bowsher.
Reality of Illusion. Exhibition catalogue, University of Southern California at Los Angeles and Denver Art Museum, Denver, Colorado. Introduction by Donald Brewer.

1980 Saint-Pierre, Adrienne E. "A Red, White, and Blue Movie." *Dialogue*, July–August, pp. 10–11.
Adams, Dennis. "Patricia Hearst: A thru Z." *So & So*, Summer–Fall, cover and p. 9.

1981 D'Agostino, Peter, and Lew Thomas, eds. *Still Photography: The Problematic Model.* San Francisco: NFS Press, pp. 111–15.

1982 Morgan, Robert C. "Book Review." *Afterimage*, November, pp. 20–21.

1983 Papenfuss, Mary. "On the West Side, Art That Stops Traffic." *Daily News* (New York), July 7, p. M3.

1984 Anderson, Susan Heller, and Maurice Carroll. "Satire in a Bus Shelter." *New York Times*, March 6, p. B4.

Meeks, Fleming. "Dennis Adams at Broadway and 66th Street." *Art in America*, September, p. 207.

Contemporary Perspectives 1984. Exhibition catalogue, Center Gallery, Bucknell University, Lewisburg, Pennsylvania. Essays by Barry Blinderman, Thomas Lawson, and Susan Morgan.

1985 "The Bus Stops Here." *New York Talk*, March, p. 20.

Adams, Dennis. "Letter to the Editor." *New Common Good*, April, p. 3.

Goldstein, Mark. "For Public Artists, New York City Is a Giant Stage." *New York Times*, April 8, p. B2.

Adams, Dennis. "Transit Authorities." *Stroll*, Spring–Summer, p. 3.

Paoletti, John T. "At the Edge Where Art Becomes Media and Message Becomes Polemic: 'Disinformation' at the Alternative Museum." *Arts Magazine*, May, pp. 132–34.

Ben-Haim, Tsipi. "New York Public Art." *International Sculpture*, June–July, p. 37.

Glueck, Grace. "Art: 'Art on the Beach,' Works and Performance." *New York Times*, July 5, p. C18.

Brenson, Michael. "What's New Around Town in Outdoor Sculpture." *New York Times*, July 19, pp. C1, C23.

Wallach, Amei. "The Last Art on the Beach." *New York Newsday*, July 19, part 3, pp. 1, 16.

Phillips, Deborah. "Bright Lights, Big City." *Artnews*, September, pp. 90–91.

Taylor, Paul. "Art on the Beach." *The Face*, September, pp. 18–19.

Garber, Stuart. "State of Mind/State of the Union." *Upfront*, Fall, pp. 14–15.

Belejack, Barbara. "The Art of Shelter." *New Manhattan Review*, November 27, p. 9.

Anderson, Susan Heller, and David Bird. "Bus Stop Exhibition." *New York Times*, December 31, p. B2.

Disinformation: The Manufacture of Consent. Exhibition catalogue, Alternative Museum, New York. Introduction by Geno Rodriguez, essays by Noam Chomsky and Edward S. Herman.

1986 Brennan, Mark. "Dennis Adams' Art at the M30." *Manhattan Arts*, April, cover and p. 2.

Kozloff, Max. "Through the Narrative Portal." *Artforum*, April, pp. 86–97.

Hardin, Terri. "Sheltering the Rosenbergs." *New York Magazine*, July 14, p. 26.

Heartney, Eleanor. "Studio: Dennis Adams." *Artnews*, October, pp. 71–72.

Brenson, Michael. "Dennis Adams at Nature Morte." *New York Times*, October 10, p. C32.

Levin, Kim. "Artwalk." *Village Voice*, October 21, p. 86.

Henderson, Justin. "Stretching the Limits." *Interiors*, November, p. 149.

Huntington, Richard. "Review: Art/An Illusive Exhibition at Hallwalls." *Buffalo News*, November 21.

Decter, Joshua. "Review." *Arts Magazine*, December, p. 124.

Heartney, Eleanor. "Art and the Electronic Fishbowl." *Artnews*, December, p. 156.

Melrod, George. "Luminous Noir: The Shades of a Scary Era." *Eye*, December, p. 35.

"Editorial: Spies Shouldn't Deface the City's Streets." *New York Post*, December 1, p. 24.

Adams, Dennis. "Questionnaire." *Zone* 1–2, pp. 423, 455.

Staniszewski, Mary Anne. "Art and About." *Manhattan, Inc.* 3, no. 8, p. 145.

The Homecoming. Exhibition catalogue, Iowa Arts Council and University of Northern Iowa, Cedar Falls, Iowa. Introduction by Bruce Williams, essays by Eleanor Heartney and Daniel E. Stetson.

Liberty and Justice. Exhibition catalogue, Alternative Museum, New York. Essays by Alexander Cockburn, Jayne Cortez, Edmund Desnoes, Benjamin R. Ringer, and Geno Rodriguez.

Uplifted Atmospheres, Borrowed Taste. Exhibition catalogue, Hallwalls, Buffalo, New York. Essay by Howard Halle.

1987 Indiana, Gary. "Dennis Adams at Nature Morte." *Art in America*, January, pp. 133–34.

Phillips, Patricia C. "Dennis Adams: Gallery Nature Morte." *Artforum*, January, p. 116.

Brenson, Michael. "Dennis Adams: Building Against Image 1979–1987." *New York Times*, January 23, p. C23.

Kazanjian, Dodie. "Portrait of the Artist 1987: Who Supports Him/Her?" Interview. *Artsreview*, Spring, pp. 63–64.

Andrew, Penelope. "Brecht on 14th Street." *New Manhattan Review*, May 20, p. 16.

Vaupel, Michael. "Zwischen Halde und Haltestelle." *Waz* (Essen), June, pp. W03–04.

Brenson, Michael. "When the Show Dwarfs the Art." *New York Times*, July 5, sec. 2, pp. 1, 25.

Hefting, Pau. "Een vragg naar de bekende weg?" *Archis*, August, pp. 8–11.

Blase, Christoph. "Die Musterschau von Münster." *Artis*, September, pp. 54–57.

Geibel, Victoria. "Capitalist Clash." *Metropolis*, September, p. 26.

Heartney, Eleanor. "Sighted in Münster." *Art in America*, September, pp. 141–43, 201.

Kuspit, Donald. "The Critic's Way: Review of *Bus Shelter IV*, Münster." *Artforum*, September, pp. 109–20.

McGill, Douglas C. "Curator of the New York City Streets." *New York Times*, September 19, p. 13.

Smolik, Noemi. "A Modest Transformation: Sculpture Project in Münster." *Vanguard*, September–October, pp. 17–19.

Engler, Brigitte. "Gimme Shelter." *Paper*, November, p. 52.

Atlantic Sculpture. Exhibition catalogue, Art Center College of Design, Pasadena, California. Introduction by Stephen Nowlin, essays by Steven Beyer, Eleanor Heartney, Joseph Masheck, and Wade Saunders.

Constitution. Exhibition catalogue, Temple Gallery, Temple University, Philadelphia. Introduction by Julie Courtney and Group Material, essays by Donald Kuspit, Michael Ratner and Margaret Ratner, and Bruce Mc.M. Wright.

Dennis Adams: Building Against Image 1979–1987. Exhibition catalogue, Alternative Museum, New York. Essay by Patricia C. Phillips, interview with the artist by Howard Halle.

Skulptur Projekte in Münster 1987. Exhibition catalogue, Westfälisches Landesmuseum, Münster, West Germany. Introduction by Klaus Bussmann and Kasper König; monographs by Klaus Bussmann, Edith Decker, Kasper König, Friedrich Meschede, Susan Weirich, and Ulrich Wilmes; essays by Thomas Kellein, Veit Loers, Christoph Schreier, Benjamin H. D. Buchloh, Hannelore Kersting, Antje von Graevenitz, Marianne Brouwer, and Gundolf Winter.

1988 Mangaliman, Jessie. "Homelessness the Theme of Artist's Show." *New York Newsday*, January 21, p. 31.
"Wo Stehen die Kunstler 1988?" *Art/Das Kunstmagazin*, February, pp. 30–47.
Costa, Vanna. "Un manipulateur d'histoire." *Beaux arts*, March, p. 93.
Phillips, Patricia C. "Adams, Jaar, Wodiczko des images parasites." *Artpress*, March, pp. 17–20.
Magnani, Gregorio. "Second Generation Post-Photography." *Flash Art*, March–April, pp. 84–87.
Brenson, Michael. "He Challenges a Privileged Point of View." *New York Times*, March 13, sec. 2, pp. 35, 38.
Tilroe, Anna. "Tralies van onbehagen." *de Volkskrant* (Amsterdam), March 25.
Wijers, Louwrien. "Dennis Adams gaat schuil in zijn wachthuisjes." *Financieel Dagblad* (Amsterdam), March 25.
Pelenc, Ariélle. "Dennis Adams: Paris, Galerie Gabrielle Maubrie." *Artefactum*, April–May, p. 48.
Rinder, Larry. "An Interview with Dennis Adams." *Artpaper*, May, pp. 9–10.
Cullinan, Helen. "Metaphor of Paranoia Caps CSU Art Season." *Plain Dealer* (Cleveland), May 14.
Poiatti, Myriam. "Genève 'retravaillée.' " *Tribune de Genève*, June 17.
"Falling Water." *Bomb*, Summer, p. 41.
Clerc, Jocelyne. "L'homme qui dérange les villes." *La femme d'aujourd'hui*, July, pp. 19–21.
Ursprung, Philip. "Reprises de vues." *NIKE: Neue Kunst in Europa*, July–August–September.
Meuris, Jacques. "Evolutions américaines actuelles." *Libre Belgique*, July 1, p. 18.
Graber, Hedy. "Bilder de Massenmedien in der Kunst." *Vaterland/Nidwaldner Volksblatt/Solothurner Nachrichten*, July 11.
Brenson, Michael. "Outdoor Sculptures Reflect Struggles of Life in the City." *New York Times*, July 15, pp. C1, C28.
B. M. "Les travailleurs étrangers nous regardent." *Tribune de Genève*, July 16.
Glueck, Grace. "An Immovable Feast: Murals in the City." *New York Times*, July 22, pp. C1, C28.
Durand, Régis. "Reprises de vues." *Artpress*, September, p. 67.
Ranzenbacher, Heimo. "Wenn aus den Abbildern neue Geschichten werden." *Steirer Krone* (Graz), September 5, p. 16.
Adams, Dennis. "Future Places." *Places*, Fall, p. 26.
Frank: An International Journal of Contemporary Writing and Art, Autumn, pp. 71, 88.
Caley, Shaun. "Special Affects: Double Takes." *Flash Art*, October, p. 140.
"Reworking Geneva." *Artpress*, October, p. 4.
Schneir, Walter, and Miriam Schneir. "Unknown Secrets." *The Guardian*, October 5, pp. 10–11.
Beurard, Patrick. "Ceci n'est pas du bri-collage." *Opus International*, November–December.
Argence, Ainardi. "Reprises de vues." *Artefactum*, November–December 1988–January 1989, pp. 50–51.
Geibel, Victoria. "Sight Specific." *Art and Auction*, November, pp. 100–108.
Hess, Elizabeth. "Captives of Industry?" *Village Voice*, November 15, p. 97.
Kohen, Helen. "Metrorail Display Lets You Hear the Visual Art." *Miami Herald*, December 7, p. 7D.
Czoppan, Gabi. "Bezugspunkte 38/88." *Kunstforum International*, no. 98, pp. 253–55.
Durand, Régis. "Dennis Adams: Une repolitisation fragile du signe." *Halle Sud*, no. 18, 2d trimester, cover and pp. 4–5.
van Duyn, Edna. "Between Innocence and Amnesia." *de Appel*, no. 2, pp. 23–26.
Bezugspunkte 38/88. Exhibition catalogue, Steirischer Herbst, Graz, Austria. Essays by Nena Dimitrijević and Werner Fenz.
Constructions: Between Sculpture and Architecture. Exhibition catalogue, Sculpture Center, New York. Essay by Frederieke Taylor.
Insight/On Site. Exhibition catalogue, Hillwood Art Gallery, C. W. Post Campus of Long Island University, Brookville, New York. Essay by Tiffany Bell.
L'inventaire/Les dimensions ordinaires. Exhibition catalogue, Manufrance, Sainte-Etienne, France. Essay by Frederic Migayrou.
Photography on the Edge. Exhibition catalogue, Haggerty Museum of Art, Marquette University, Milwaukee, Wisconsin. Essays by Noel Carroll and Curtis L. Carter.
Politically Charged. Exhibition catalogue, First Street Forum, Saint Louis, Missouri. Essay by Judy Van Wagner.
Presi x incantamento: La nuova fotografia internazionale. Exhibition catalogue, Padiglione d'Arte Contemporanea, Milan. Introduction by Gregorio Magnani, essays by Daniela Salvioni and Giorgio Verzotti.
Reprises de vues. Exhibition catalogue, Halle Sud, Geneva. Introduction by Renate Cornu, essay by Corinne Diserens.
The Whole World Is Still Watching. Exhibition catalogue, Randolph Street Gallery, Chicago. Essays by Dan Mills and Maureen Sherlock.
Modern Dreams: The Rise and Fall and Rise of Pop Art. Boston: Institute of Contemporary Art; New York: The Clocktower; and Cambridge: MIT Press, pp. 6, 11, 110–13, 115–17.
Okun, Rob A. *The Rosenbergs: Collected Visions of Artists and Writers*. New York: Universe Books, pls. 50, 51.
1989 Ledes, Richard C. "Dennis Adams, Alfredo Jaar, Jeff Wall: Tomoko Liguori Gallery." *Artforum*, January, pp. 113–14.
Durand, Régis. "Politiques de l'image." *Beaux arts*, January, pp. 44–49.
Brenson, Michael. "Dennis Adams: John Weber Gallery." *New York Times*, January 27, p. C17.
Schwartzman, Allan. "Public Art: Corporate Trophies." *Art in America*, February, pp. 34–43.
Gattinoni, Christian. "Les fictions critiques de la photographie." *Artension*, March, pp. 42–43.
Tarantino, Michael. "Gallery Round Up." *The Bulletin* (Brussels), March 16, p. 11.
Meuris, Jacques. "Questionnements, Presque Toujours." *Libre Belgique*, March 17.
Lambrecht, Luk. "Kunst-Provocatie." *Knackweekend* (Brussels), March 22, p. 17.
Heartney, Eleanor. "Street Scenes." *Art in America*, April, pp. 230–37, 277.
Lambrecht, Luk. "Images Critiques." *Artefactum*, April–May, pp. 44–45.
Brenson, Michael. "Juxtaposing the New from All Over." *New York Times*, May 20, pp. 11, 12.
Douthat, Anita. "Transforming with Light." *Art New England*, June, pp. 10–11, 29.
Bobka, Vivian. "Dennis Adams: Christine Burgin." *Flash Art*, Summer, pp. 148–49.
Sans, Jerôme. "Dennis Adams." Interview. *Flash Art*, Summer, pp. 129–31.

Geer, Suvan. "Margo Leavin Gallery." *Los Angeles Times*, June 23, pp. 14–15.
Heartney, Eleanor. "The New Social Sculpture." *Sculpture*, July–August, pp. 24–27, 49.
Tamir, Tali. "The Present Station of Dennis Adams." *Kol-Hair* (Jerusalem), July 7, pp. 58–59, 71.
Shaked, Shlomit. "Memorial War in Oblivion." *Ma'ariv* (Tel Aviv), July 21.
Manor, Dalia. "Dennis Adams Bus-Stop." *Ha-aretz* (Tel Aviv), August, pp. 28–29.
Lepage, Jocelyne. "De la photographie au deuxième degré." *La Presse* (Montreal), August 12, p. D8.
Campbell, James. "Tenir l'image à distance." *C Magazine*, September, pp. 80–81.
Phillips, Patricia C. "Dennis Adams: Christine Burgin Gallery." *Artforum*, September, pp. 142–43.
Rubin, Jane. "Margo Leavin Gallery." *Art Issues*, September–October, p. 23.
Wilson, Andrew. "Dennis Adams: Galerie Meert-Rihoux." *Artscribe International*, September–October, pp. 91–92.
Bourriaud, Nicolas. "Magiciens de la Terre." *Flash Art*, October, pp. 118–21.
Moorman, Margaret. "Dennis Adams at Christine Burgin." *Artnews*, October, p. 197.
Laframboise, Alain. "Tenir l'image à distance." *Parachute*, October–November–December, pp. 52–53.
"1. Internationale Foto-Triennale Esslingen 1989." *Kunstmagazin ZYMA*, November–December, pp. 74–77.
McCracken, David. "Photography's Past, Present and Future." *Chicago Tribune*, November 24, sec. 7, p. 68.
Oleksijczuk, Denise. "Publics Art." *File Megazine* (Toronto), no. 29, pp. 49–61.
1. Internationale Foto-Triennale. Exhibition catalogue, Villa Merkel, Esslingen, West Germany. Essays by Alexander Tolnay, Ute Eskildsen, Els Barents, Christine Frisinghelli, Mark Haworth-Booth, and Manfred Schmalriede.
Conspicuous Display. Exhibition catalogue, Stedman Art Gallery, Rutgers University, Camden, New Jersey. Essay by Sid Sachs.
D & S Ausstellung. Exhibition catalogue, Kunstverein Hamburg. Essays by Frank Barth, Thomas Wulffen, Michael Haerdter, Dietmas Kamper, Michael Lingner, S. D. Sauerbier, Jürgen Schwienebraden, and Freiherr von Wichman-Eichhorn.
Image World: Art and Media Culture. Exhibition catalogue, Whitney Museum of American Art, New York. Essays by Lisa Phillips, Marvin Heiferman, and John Hanhardt.
Images Critiques: Adams, Jaar, Jammes, Wall. Exhibition catalogue, L'ARC, Musée d'Art Moderne de la Ville de Paris. Introduction by Suzanne Pagé, essays by Béatrice Parent and Ariélle Pelenc.
Magiciens de la Terre. Exhibition catalogue, Centre Georges Pompidou and La Grande Halle, Parc La Villette, Paris. Essays by Jean-Hubert Martin, Aline Luque, Mark Francis, André Magnin, Pierre Gaudibert, Thomas McEvilley, Homi Bhabda, Jacques Soulillou, and Bernard Marcarde.
The Photography of Invention: American Pictures of the 1980s. Exhibition catalogue, National Museum of American Art, Smithsonian Institution, Washington, D.C. Introduction by Merry Foresta, essay by Joshua Smith.
Public Art Program 1985–1988. Brookville, New York: Hillwood Art Gallery, C. W. Post Campus of Long Island University.
Sequence (Con)Sequence: (Sub)Versions of Photography in the 80s. Exhibition catalogue, Edith C. Blum Art Institute, Bard College, Annandale-on-Hudson, New York. Essays by Julia Ballerini, William S. Wilson, and Lori Zippay.
Tenir l'image à distance. Exhibition catalogue, Musée d'Art Contemporain, Montreal. Essay by Réal Lussier.
Duval, Adele, and Dennis Adams. *Public Difference*. New York: Christine Burgin Gallery.
Magnani, Gregorio, Daniela Salvioni, and Giorgio Verzotti. *Special Effects: The Photographic Experience in Contemporary Art*. Milan: Giancarlo Politi Editore, pp. 13, 25–27, 162, 165, 191.
Plagemann, Volker, ed. *Kunst im öffentlichen Raum*. Cologne: DuMont Buchverlag, pp. 125, 129, 142, 148, 242.

Palm-Zigarren
Palm-Zigarren

KENT

41 East 57 Street, New York, NY 10022

This monograph accompanies the exhibition *Dennis Adams: Street Vanities* held at Kent Fine Art, April 5 to May 5, 1990

Edited by Susan Harris
Designed by Tony Morgan, New York
Type set in New Caledonia and Helvetica by Trufont Typographers, New York
Text paper: Warren's Lustro Dull
Printed by Becker Graphics, New York
First printing, 3000 copies

Photography by Dennis Adams, unless otherwise captioned

Archive photos:
Associated Press
Black Star
Bettmann Archive, UPS & Reuter
Paul Glaser
Paris Match
Landesmuseum Joanneum
Landesbildstelle Berlin
Ullstein Bilderdienst

ISBN 1-878607-07-3